MW01051148

SOUL-WINNING

IS EASY

C. S. Lovett

SOUL WINNING IS EASY

by
C. S. LOVETT, M.A., B.D.

ZONDERVAN PUBLISHING HOUSE
OF THE ZONDERVAN CORPORATION
GRAND RAPIDS, MICHIGAN 49506

Soul-Winning Is Easy

Copyright 1954 by C. S. Lovett

First Zondervan printing 1957
Twenty-sixth printing 1979
ISBN 0-310-28401-5

Printed in the United States of America

MOST FAMILIES FIND IT EASY TO TALK ABOUT CHRIST BUT FEW
EVER INTRODUCE ANYONE TO HIM.

FOREWORD

There are many Christians who can sit around the living-room, spending an afternoon or evening extolling the advantages of the Christian life, but there are very few who are skillful in making the introduction of a soul to Christ. As in everything else, we enjoy doing those things that we can do well, while we shun those things we find difficult. The matter of presenting Christ is as simple and easy as any other introduction and with a little practice and a method the average Christian can bring anyone face to face with the Lord Jesus. Mastering the basic principles and the techniques set forth here will give the personal worker confidence and joy in serving in this most rewarding ministry. In the space of a short time the average Christian can be an "expert" Soul-Winner, present himself to the Lord for this work, and then have the supreme joy of leading many to Him.

Much has been written on the subject of soul-winning, but little of it gives practical help in the art of "closing the deal" — it is at this point of the "close in" where Christians need strengthening and skill.

It is with this in mind that these instructions are presented to you, for they are designed to give you the needed skill and confidence in your soul-winning. The writer is not presenting this system as an author or scholar, but as a servant of Christ, desiring only to place this tool in the hands of Christians. No system can save souls — that is the work of the Saviour — therefore, to be used in this work, both the winner and his system must be presented to the Lord for His service.

It is to the Lord Jesus Christ that this work is dedicated, for it is He that has imparted this skill to His servants.

C. S. LOVETT

Pastor
Baldwin Park Baptist Church
Baldwin Park, California

The <u>HEART</u> of this system is the <u>PERSON</u> of Jesus Christ.

The <u>REQUISITE</u> of this system is knowing that <u>PERSON</u>.

The <u>OBJECT</u> of this system is to bring an individual "Face to Face" with the <u>PERSON</u> of Jesus Christ and to invite the individual to <u>RECEIVE</u> that <u>PERSON</u>!

INTRODUCING CHRIST TO A PERSON IS THE SAME AS ANY OTHER
INTRODUCTION.

SOUL WINNING IS EASY

*   *   *   *   *   *

INTRODUCTION

The receiving of Christ is a <u>PERSONAL</u> transaction that takes place between an individual and God. It is the failure to recognize that Salvation consists of <u>re</u>ceiving a <u>PERSON</u> that fills our churches with *professors* rather than *possessors*.

<u>THEREFORE</u>:   <u>Keep in mind always that you are presenting a PERSON</u>! The introducing of a person to Christ is the same as any other introduction —

> Ill: Today we say, "John Jones, I'd like to have you meet Bill Smith". Only in soul-winning we say, "I'd like to have you know Jesus Christ who has done a wonderful thing for you". It's true that Jesus does not have a visible body for one to see neither is a visible hand extended for one to grasp, but none the less His presence is made to be just as real as anyone else's by the Holy Spirit.

Perhaps this is the place to point out that it is the Holy Spirit who makes Christ real to a person and not us—we simply make the introduction because the Holy Spirit, has already made Christ real to us. Having made the introduction, there will be some response from the person to whom Jesus has been introduced. If we introduce one person to another there is always some response; a "how-do-you-do" or "happy to know you," or it is possible that one might blurt out, "I don't want to know you!", but always there is some response. If the introduction has actually been made there will be an awareness of it. This awareness takes the form of a *decision.* "Do I want Christ for my friend or don't I?" If the introduction is real, Christ will be counted as a friend or regarded as an enemy.

THE SOUL-WINNER A SALESMAN

Since the soul-winner is somewhat a salesman for Jesus Christ, much is to be gained from observing the determined manner in which the clever, worldly salesman brings a customer to a decision concerning his product.

Ill: All of us have had the experience of having a salesman call at our home and during the presentation talk he begins to fill in a contract form, often asking such questions as "how many in your family?"—"You would need about five, wouldn't you?" All the while he makes entries on the contract form, even before you have agreed to buy his product. Before long the contract is filled out and he hands it to you with a pen and says, "Here, would you approve this?" or "Would you

THE CLEVER, WORLDLY SALESMAN NEVER FAILS TO BRING YOU TO A DECISION CONCERNING HIS PRODUCT.

just sign here?" There is no idle bantering of words now, you must accept or reject — you make a *clear decision* — "Yes or No."

The effective soul-winner will, in the same way, bring an individual to the place where he will say, "Come into my heart, Lord Jesus!" *or* "Go away, I don't want your salvation!" Anything short of this is simply not presenting Christ. A person does not have to say, "Go away, Lord Jesus!" in order to be a rejecter of Christ; to fail to receive Him is as though one said, "Go away." There is no middle ground. "He that is not with Me is against Me." (Matt. 12:30).

WARNING

Satan will try every means to get you off the track. Usually some question is asked about a subject with which you are quite familiar, but the opportunity it affords you to show off your knowledge of the Bible must be passed up. You are there for only one purpose, and you must stay "on the target!" Think back now, in your own experience, how many times has Satan used this method to keep you from presenting the most vital matter, that of an individual's salvation?

This next is very difficult. Regardless of the criticism that a person makes against the Bible—DISREGARD IT COMPLETELY! The Bible is the LIVING Word of God and in the hands of the Holy Spirit it becomes a SWORD

DON'T DEFEND THE WORD OF GOD!

USE IT!!

Ill: If an intruder attempted to enter your home, and the safety of your family was threatened, you might defend them with a gun, but you wouldn't say to the intruder, "This is a Colt .45, it holds six bullets and when I press the trigger a process of combustion takes place in the barrel which will discharge a lead pellet, killing you!" No—*You wouldn't explain or defend the gun—you would use it!*

It is just as ridiculous to defend the Sword of the Spirit." Don't be afraid to trust it—it is "quick and powerful!" If you don't believe God will honor His Word—don't try to use it.

Ill: The writer has had the experience of presenting Jesus in the Word time and again. Often different ones would say, "I don't believe that!" or "How do you know that this is true?" or "Man wrote that anyway!" Their protests were ignored as though they were never uttered and in the course of a few minutes tears were streaming down their faces as they invited Jesus to come into their hearts.

The one disclaiming the Bible as God's Word is arguing with God and not with you. As you speak, the Holy Spirit is constantly bearing witness to the truth.

IT IS FOOLISH TO DEFEND YOUR WEAPON; RATHER YOU WOULD
USE IT.

YOUR TOOLS WILL INCLUDE YOUR TESTAMENT, A BLANK CARD,
B-RATIONS, A GOSPEL OF JOHN, AND THE PAMPHLET.

The subject will have to decide whether he will listen to God or not and always there is that awareness of the awful fact of calling God a liar. You cannot depend upon the words that come from his lips as revealing what he honestly feels within his heart, for so convicting is the presence of God's truth, that the subject will unhesitatingly speak untrue words as a device to silence your witness.

God's Word is "quick and powerful, and sharper than any twoedged sword . . ." (Heb. 4:12) The fact that people do not believe the Bible has nothing to do with the effectiveness of the Word itself. It is not necessary for one to believe the Bible for it to become the voice of God speaking to his heart. We become God's lips and His Spirit makes the message living and real.

THE TOOLS YOU'LL NEED

1. A THIN 6" NEW TESTAMENT

The American Bible Society has an inexpensive one that is just about the right size, for it will conveniently fit a ladies purse or the back pocket of a man's trousers. You want your Bible to be of a size that it can easily be concealed on your person. The sight of a Bible under your arm can sometimes be very frightening and often creates apprehensions and barriers that are not easily overcome. The writer of Proverbs tells us that "Surely in vain the net is spread in the sight of any bird" (1:17). While the displaying of a Bible may at other times be a testimony, it is usually a hindrance in soul-winning.

TABS are most helpful on the edges of the pages which bear the references that you will be using. A little strip of cellophane tape is sufficient, or any idea that is most suitable for you, so that you can turn to the reference quickly without having to search for it. You will want to keep the conversation going in the meantime and long periods of searching for the Scripture reference produce awkwardness. Any delay while you are looking for your place provides opportunity for the subject to introduce questions or protests which are foreign to the purpose of the moment. You do not want them to get off the subject for a single moment, and the smoothness with which you carry out your transition from step to step is vital to this end.

When you have turned to the reference by means of the TAB, be sure that the page is free from any distracting markings. It is best to keep your little New Testament just for this purpose alone and use another for personal study. Pages that are cluttered with notes and symbols are a hindrance to the subject in trying to locate the verse you are quoting. Not only should the pages be kept clean, but the four verses that are used in the system should be underlined in red so that the eyes of the subject will quickly pick up the reference.

2. BLANK CARDS

Keep a blank 3" x 5" card in your New Testament so

that it will be handy for the illustrations. This is a most important tool. Carry extra blank cards in your pocket on which you can write down names and addresses for follow-up. The cards, you will find, are also useful in keeping the corners of tracts nice and straight while you are carrying them in your pocket.

3. HELPS TO LEAVE WITH THE NEW CHRISTIAN

Salvation Clear and Plain—This is a suitable leaflet to leave in his hands after you have dealt with him, which will explain the salvation he has just received, for he will not be able to remember everything that you have said to him; as a matter of fact he will know little more than the fact that he has just made a decision to trust Christ as Saviour. This booklet by Dr. William Orr, *Salvation Clear and Plain* can be secured from Christian Supply.

The Gospel of John—written on good quality paper such as the one put out by the Pocket Testament League. This one is good because it has the pertinent verses boxed in red and the decision page at the back is convenient for him to write down the date and keep it to remember the day that he was "born again."

"B-Rations"—A convenient packet containing a review of the new Christian's experience and the thoughts Satan will challenge him with as soon as he has left your strengthening fellowship. Only the Word can answer Satan's implanted doubts, and four Scripture verses on separate cards are included for the "Babe" to memorize for assurance and defense against the first thrusts of the enemy. These aids can **all** be secured from Christian Supply, Baldwin Park, Calif.

CONTROLLING THE CONVERSATION

The advantage of using a system is that you know what you are going to do and say each step of the way. After a little practice you will find that not only do you know what you are going to say, but you will also know what the subject's reply will be to your questions. You will discover that you control the conversation by your questions and your explanations of the Scripture passages. It is important that you do control the conversation, so that you can keep the subject focused on the issue all the time. You are there to present Christ and to show the individual his need of Christ. By controlling the conversation you keep unrelated materials from being introduced into the discussion—you keep the subject's mind on the central thing—and you enjoy the confidence of being able to bring the subject to a decision in a very short time. If the subject should get in a question, it is best not to answer it at all. Ignore it if possible; and if not, tell him you will answer it in a moment, but that you wish him to see a certain point first. Today, all good salesmen are trained to control the conversation. You'll find this very easy to do when you know your system well.

THE APPROACH

There are three questions that may be used with real psychological force. Normally they would be used in succession, but circumstances may dictate that you omit the first and even possibly the second. After a little experience you will be able to determine easily what is needed in each situation.

1. "ARE YOU INTERESTED IN SPIRITUAL THINGS?"

Notice there is not a bit of offense in this question. Its psychological force stems from the fact that few people are willing to confess that they have no interest in spiritual things. Sometimes they answer,

"Oh, sure," or again, "I believe in God"; "I go to church."

Regardless of their answer the next question is easily in order.

2. "HAVE YOU EVER THOUGHT OF BECOMING A CHRISTIAN?"

This question carries a bit more weight with it. Your attitude and tone of voice is of special importance from now on. Be sweet and unassuming or there will be offense. You won't have to speak authoritatively just yet because of the force of the question. He will show some reaction to this question because of its psychological implication. Now notice that this question assumes that the individual is unsaved. It puts him in the

—19—

place of having to make a declaration for Christ if he wants you to believe otherwise. This is just exactly what our attitude should be toward anyone unless we have evidence to the contrary. It is a most unkind thing to assume anyone's salvation. To satisfy yourself on the force of this question, try asking individuals, "Are you a Christian?" and you will observe that they practically always say, "Yes." That is because, in this country almost everyone assumes that if he is not born of a Jewish family, and doesn't practice the heathen worship of darkest Africa, he automatically must be a Christian. He reasons, "After all, isn't America a Christian land?"

But when you place the burden on him of having to come out and say in defense of himself, "Why, I __AM__ a Christian!", that is not so easy. Usually it is only the "born again" believer that will say this.

The answer to your question, "Have you ever thought of becoming a Christian?" is generally,

"No, not much," or "I've thought about it," or
"I used to go to Sunday School."

If the person is a genuine Christian he will not mind answering the question, but it does force the non-Christian to declare his stand in relation to Christ. With just one question you gain much insight to his true spiritual condition.

3. "SUPPOSE SOMEONE WERE TO ASK YOU, 'WHAT IS A CHRISTIAN', WHAT WOULD YOU SAY?"

This question employs the greatest amount of psychology and observe that it makes your question seem quite impersonal. It is as though someone else were asking the question. The question is quite direct, and yet the sharpness is removed by phrasing it, "Suppose someone were to ask you." In a sense you have transferred the question to a hypothetical person and it is as though another were putting the subject on the "spot" instead of you. Here you must be sweet, gently couching your words in mellow tones. A twinkle in your eye as you speak, and gentleness, will go a long way in removing still more of the tension that might otherwise spring up within the subject.

NOTE: Your third approach question can be adapted to the situation. If you're in a man's store, it would be well to say, "Suppose a customer were to ask . . .?", or again, if you are in someone's home you could easily ask, "Suppose your child (or relative) were to ask, 'What is a Christian?' what would you say?" It is best to have a set approach while you are beginning, but as you gain experience you will find that your effectiveness can be increased by tailoring your style to meet the circumstances.

In response to your question, the answer that generally comes back is: "Well, it's someone who believes in God and does the best he can."

You say: "Yes, it's true that a Christian does that, or at least tries to, BUT what IS a Christian?"

He'll answer: "Well, one who goes to church, and prays . . . etc."

Again you will say: "Yes, that's true, a Christian does all these things, but just what IS he?" "He's different from all other people for he has something that no one else has—can you think what that might be?"

It won't matter what his answer is, for you can always counter with: "Yes, a Christian does that, but what is a Christian?"

Even if he says, "Someone who believes in Christ," your reply would still be the same: "Yes, a Christian does believe in Christ, but what is he?" Though he says a Christian is one who believes in Christ, he will generally mean one who believes about Christ and so your answer would still be the same. Regardless of his answer, purpose to go all the way through the plan, for it is impossible to determine his true condition until after you have delivered the final invitation.

You continue the process of asking the question, usually three or four times is sufficient, until he is exhausted of answers. At this point you can see that he is perplexed—generally he will pause, thinking seriously, for he has become aware of the fact that he does not know the answer and hence must not be a Christian himself. It's obvious, of course, that he cannot tell someone something that he himself does not know.

Now notice what you have been doing by this type of questioning.

1. You are emphasizing the fact that a Christian _is_ something, rather than someone that _does_ something. The average person feels that a Christian is one who _does_ certain things, rather than **being** something in himself.

2. With just a few remarks you have gained tremendous insight into his understanding of spiritual things—and can now discern how best to meet his need.

3. You have allowed the individual to show himself that he is not a Christian.

4. You have placed him in the position of having to tell you what is in his heart, rather than your merely lecturing in words, so many of which are lost.

5. You have caused him to concentrate upon the matter, and indirectly to think upon his own need, since people always see themselves in everything.

6. And very important, you have exhausted him—a thing which will keep him silent as you present the plan of Salvation. It is always wise to let a subject "run down" first, before you speak, as any psychologist will tell you; and here it is especially helpful in that it prevents interruptions.

WARNING:

Never at any time during the questioning should you say, in response to his answer, "No, that's not what a Christian is, he is . . . .", and then proceed to tell him what a Christian is. You'll find that you have merely given away information which the subject will turn around in a few seconds and give back to you, thereby thwarting your plan. Just wait, for when it comes time to tell him what a Christian is, you'll be using the Word!

As you come to the end of your questioning (actually it takes just a few seconds) the subject says:

"I don't know—what is a Christian? You tell me." Sometimes there is a pause during which the subject says nothing, and it becomes readily apparent from the look on his face that he is now exhausted, not knowing what to say next. Having reached this point, he is usually quite ready to listen to what you have to say— as a matter of fact he has to be quiet—for it is true that one simply cannot tell you something that he does not know. This is of the greatest advantage for he will not be interrupting you to tell you what *he* believes as you present the plan.

NOW YOU ARE READY TO USE THE WORD

Before you reach for the New Testament that has been concealed, you say, "With your permission I'd like to read four verses of Scripture and explain them to you, then you'll know what a Christian is!" This sounds simple and innocent enough. Surely four verses

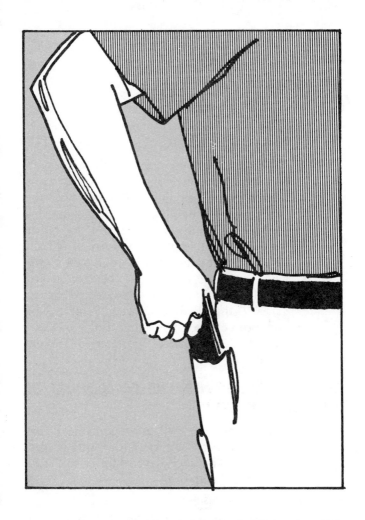

AT THE RIGHT MOMENT YOUR TESTAMENT IS QUICKLY PRODUCED
FROM ITS PLACE OF CONCEALMENT.

shouldn't take too long, and most people will either say, "Go ahead" or "Okay."

THE PRESENTATION

Quickly produce from your pocket the New Testament, saying (as you turn to the first reference) "God says that we are all sinners, as we see here in Romans 3:23."

> HINT: Your tabs assist you to turn to the place with one simple motion of your hand. Stand to one side of the subject and, if possible, hold the Word in front of him. This makes the discussion between the individual and God rather than between him and you; further, it fixes his eyes on the Word, and your own words will carry more intimacy as they are spoken directly into his ear. The eye gate and the ear gate are thus both employed. Point to the underscored verse with your finger, as you read, to further direct his attention to the Word.

"FOR ALL HAVE SINNED AND COME SHORT OF THE GLORY OF GOD"

You: "God says that we are all in the same boat, that we are all sinners. We know that this is true, don't we? For instance, have you ever told a lie . . . in all of your life?"

Subject: "Sure, who hasn't?"

You: "We all have, haven't we? Well then, how many lies does it take to make a liar?"

YOUR TESTAMENT HELD IN FRONT OF THE SUBJECT CONFRONTS HIM
WITH GOD'S WORD.

ONE FINGER HELD BELOW THE LINE OF VISION AUTOMATICALLY
ANSWERS, "HOW MANY LIES DOES IT TAKE TO MAKE A LIAR?"

"IF JESUS WERE STANDING ALONGSIDE . . . " POINT TO THE PLACE.

HINT: At this point hold up one finger just below his line of vision, and yet conspicuous enough to be seen. It is so strongly suggestive that he will always answer, "Just one, I suppose!"

Now ask: "If the Lord Jesus were standing alongside of you right now (point to the location) would you say that you were as righteous as He?"

Subject: "No, of course not!"

You: "Why not?"

Subject: "Well, I'm just not."

You: "No, and that is what God has just said. We <u>are</u> sinners, and we <u>do</u> come short of His glory."

NOTE: All you're trying to show in this step is that the subject is a sinner—as soon as he is convinced of this, move on.

Quickly open to <u>Romans 6:23.</u>

You: "Our sin has earned something for us. Because we are sinners God says that we've earned certain wages." Point to the passage as you read aloud—

"THE WAGES OF SIN IS DEATH, BUT THE GIFT OF GOD IS ETERNAL LIFE THROUGH JESUS CHRIST OUR LORD."

You: "Here God says that the wages for our sin is death and we've already seen that we have earned them. This means that because of our sin we have earned death."

NOTE: If you feel some comment is necessary upon

the word *death,* you can say, "Death is separation; physical death is the separation of the soul from the body, and spiritual death is the separation of the soul from God. God says that our sin has brought about separation and it is eternal."

Continue: "In the state of California, if you work for a man and have wages coming, the law says that those wages must be paid. God's law says that since we've sinned, the wages of our sin must be paid. And we can be sure that they will be paid for His law is far more exacting than that of the State of California."

You: "As sinners, then, either we must receive those wages or someone must receive them for us. That is what Christ did on the cross 2000 years ago. In His death He received full payment for all your sin.Now listen to what God says. He's not talking about death any longer, but the very opposite, 'LIFE' — 'ETERNAL LIFE' — as a gift." (Read this last portion of the verse again, pointing to the passage).

"BUT THE <u>GIFT</u> OF GOD IS <u>ETERNAL LIFE</u> THROUGH ('IN' - ASV) JESUS CHRIST OUR LORD"

You: "Here we see that God is talking about a gift— that he has a gift for us (pause). "You can't earn a gift, can you? You don't pay for a gift." (Shake your head negatively).

Subject's response: "No."

You: "That's true, we cannot __earn__ a gift. All that anyone can do with a gift is *accept* it or *reject* it.
Here God tells us that He is offering us eternal
life as a free gift. That means that we don't
get it by being good or bad, or by going to
church, or by being baptized, or anything else—
but merely by receiving it as a __free__ __gift__.

NOTE: From this point on you will use many questions and repetitions. Educators tell us that
points have to be repeated as many as thirty
times before they are learned by students in
the public school systems.

You: "We've seen that God has a gift for us, and what
did we say that gift was?"

Subject: "Eternal life."

You: "And now we see __where__ it is. It is __in__ a Person. It's
a free gift, the gift is eternal life, and it's in a
Person. Let me demonstrate with this card."

Ill: Hold the blank card up in your hand and say,
" Let's imagine that this card is five dollars and
I want to give it to you as a gift (sometimes
you can relax some tensions by saying, 'I wish
it were five dollars'), but I put it in this book
(your New Testament) first and then hand it
to you like this—why, you'd take the book to
get the five dollars, wouldn't you?"

NOTE: Make your motions slowly and deliberately,
placing the card in the book at the same time
you say the words, "But I put it in this book."

"LET'S IMAGINE THAT THIS CARD IS FIVE DOLLARS."

"BUT I PUT IT IN THIS BOOK."

"YOU'D TAKE THE BOOK TO GET THE FIVE DOLLARS."

Then offer the book to him with the card protruding from the end. It isn't necessary for him to take the book from your hand, for all you're trying to show at this point is that the gift is *in a container*—that is, in Christ.

You: "This gift that God has for us is *in* Christ, and just as you'd take the book from my hand to get the five dollars, in the same way you must take Christ to get the gift of eternal life, because the gift is in Him. And that is what God tells us in John 1:12—that we need to <u>receive</u> Christ."

NOTE: Again the use of your tabs will enable you to turn swiftly to the reference.

Repeat: "Remember, we've said it is a free gift—that the gift is eternal life—that it is in Christ—and that we need to receive Him in order to get it. Now listen . . ."

"BUT AS MANY AS <u>RECEIVED HIM</u> TO THEM GAVE HE POWER TO BECOME THE SONS OF GOD."

You: "Here God says we need to <u>receive</u> Christ in order to become His children. Today our churches are filled with people who believe a lot <u>about</u> Christ, such as His virgin birth, miracles, and even death and resurrection; but, they still will never make heaven, because they've never <u>received</u> Christ. There's a big difference between <u>be-lieving</u> and <u>receiving</u> (pause briefly). Let me demonstrate what I mean with this card."

NOTE: Now take your blank 3 x 5 card again and hold it up just out of reach of the subject, but as though offering it to him.

Now say: "I offer you this card as a free gift—you believe me, don't you?"

Subject: Usually he will hesitate and then utter a cautious "Yes."

HINT: If he seems fearful to reply, you can allay his fears with, "There's no trick. I just want to illustrate the difference between believing and receiving"—then he will relax and say, "Yes, I believe you."

Now ask him: "But do you have it?"

Subject: "No, not yet."

You: "Here I offer it to you as a free gift—you believe me—and yet you do not have it, do you?"

Subject: "No."

You: "Why not—I've offered it to you?"

NOTE: He may answer: "Because I didn't take it." This is fine if he does, but most often the subject will be thinking and the answer won't come to him right away. Don't wait for it— pause briefly, and then continue.

You: "All right, now reach out your hand and take it right out of my hand. (Subject does so). Now you have it, don't you? You received it—you know that you have it in your own possession." (Generally he nods his head in reply for he is

"I OFFER YOU THIS CARD AS A GIFT—YOU BELIEVE ME, DON'T YOU?"

"ALL RIGHT, NOW REACH OUT YOUR HAND AND TAKE IT RIGHT OUT OF MY HAND."

"AS LONG AS IT WAS IN MY HAND . . ." AS YOU SAY THESE
WORDS, RETRIEVE THE CARD.

usually thinking over the step—a dramatic participation always causes more thought than mere words).

NOTE: As you speak the next words, reach forward with your hand and retrieve the card from his fingers.

You: "As long as it was in my hand, like this (now it is back in your hand and you hold it up), no matter how much you believed, you didn't have it, did you?"

Subject: "No."

NOTE: The primary reason this verse is used is to show that God's gift must be received. "Received is the key word here! The word "believe has a variety of meanings today, none of which come close to the New Testament idea of full commitment to Christ. For that reason, in the matter of Salvation, it is better to use "receive," for here the meaning is unquestionable.

You: "In the same way, we need to receive Christ. Just as you took the card that I offered to you, so also must you take the gift that God offers to you (brief pause). And here's how you do it. (Turn to Revelation 3:20 while talking). Now remember that we have seen that God has a free gift—that the gift is eternal life—and that it is in a person, Jesus Christ—and to get the gift we must receive that Person. Now listen carefully, for this is THE LORD JESUS SPEAK-ING TO YOU!" (These exact words are important for they convey to the subject's heart that Jesus is speaking and not you. Also the subject is prepared for what follows).

NOTE: Now we are moving into that portion of the plan which requires you to act with the full authority of the "Great Commission." Be bold and firm, for it is at this point that most Christians drop out of the race. As you tell him that this is the Lord Jesus speaking to him, look the subject squarely in the eye, and unwaveringly speak as Christ's Ambassador with the certain authority that is given to you by God.

Even though God has given us the authority to speak boldly in His name, we must never forget that Jesus is the real Soul-Winner—as a matter of fact, "Jesus does it all." All of our techniques—all of our skill—any psychology we might use—are absolutely worthless unless they are fully surrendered to the Holy Spirit and used as His tools. Our Lord's own counsel in this matter is, "Without Me ye can do nothing." His authority is our authority as long as it is Christ working through us.

"BEHOLD I STAND AT THE DOOR AND KNOCK: IF ANY MAN HEAR MY VOICE, AND OPEN THE DOOR, I-WILL-COME-IN . . ."

NOTE: Leave off the remainder of the verse. Otherwise it will be necessary to explain the oriental meaning of "sup" and its connotation of lifetime fellowship, which is wonderful to consider, but doesn't aid in the decision at this moment. If the subject asks about it, just say that it means "fellowship" and get right back to the decision. Read the verse slowly, emphasizing the underlined portions.

You: "The Lord says, *'Behold, I stand at the door'* — that *door* is the door of your heart."

HINT: As you tell him that the "door" is the door of his heart, reach over and tap on his heart or shoulder. This suddenly shatters his "dream of words" making the situation dramatically real.

You: "Notice he says, 'If any man hear My voice and open the door' (pause). Who opens the door? Man opens the door! Any man! Anybody! If anyone will open that door, He says, 'I will come in'. Even though He's the Lord of all Glory— the Maker of Heaven and Earth, He stands at the door of a human heart as if He had no power at all—just knocking and awaiting an invitation to come in. You see, you have a free-will, and no one can make you believe anything you don't want to believe. It can't be done because God made you that way, and He himself won't force that door open. He won't violate your free-will.

"THAT DOOR IS THE DOOR OF YOUR HEART."

ONE WOULDN'T HESITATE TO SAY, "COME IN" WERE A FRIEND
KNOCKING AT THE DOOR.

Though He has all power, He humbly knocks, as if He had none, (tap on your Bible) waiting for you to open the door." (Pause—lower your voice—speak directly—make it warm and intimate).

"If I were a good friend of yours, Bill, (use the first name of the subject if possible) and came over to your house and wanted to come in and knocked at the door—(rap on Bible) what would you say?"

Subject: "I'd say, 'Come in'."

THIS IS THE CRUCIAL POINT — DON'T WAVER HERE! — HERE'S WHERE SKILL IS NEEDED!

You: "The Lord Jesus is waiting to come into your heart right now,—will you tell Him to come in? Will you open the door of your heart?" (Pause briefly, a maximum of 3 seconds, while you wait for his answer).

NOTE: If you wait too long for his answer at this point, it can cause trouble. Satan is working furiously at this stage—this is the vital moment—everything that you have said was to bring the subject to this point of decision. A question interjected now may seriously remove the subject's mind from the decision that he is facing. Be bold, and keep your own heart stayed on Christ; be conscious of your own weakness, and at the same time of His mighty power; pray in the "inner man" for the subject's salvation even while you're speaking, and at the right moment, the Holy Spirit will guide you in pressing for the decision.

EXPLANATION:

You may think that what you are about to read next is too much high pressure. But remember you are giving all that you have to Christ for the Salvation of this soul. It is important to be *wise as serpents and harmless as doves* as you assist the subject in his decision. Every pressure is being applied to keep him from making this decision. His heart is a battle ground. The "door" that he is to open is rusted shut, and Satan <u>does not</u> want it opened. But the Holy Spirit is desirous that the door be opened, and He will employ every available means to accomplish this end. Our efforts, skills, and techniques are but *means* placed in His hands. You, as a personal worker, have joined forces with the Holy Spirit in this battle, and you are now serving as a "co-laborer" in the work of opening that "rusted" door. The personal worker is in the front lines, actually encountering the enemy, as many a <u>well used</u> Saint can testify. This is why many are not willing to give themselves to this type of ministry and also why many drop by the way side long before a subject has come to the place of actual decision. As you give yourself to this type of a ministry, you will find that there will be much criticism coming from those who are content to stay behind the lines, but be assured that the "Victor's" crown will be adorned by

His praise, "well done!"

<u>Remember</u>, no matter how much effort you expend or what techniques you use, it will be the Holy Spirit that gives him the grace to make his own decision. Your efforts will serve to reduce his fleshly resistance. The Spirit's work will meet the need of his heart.

HERE'S HOW TO PRESS FOR THE DECISION

Lay your hand firmly on the subject's arm or shoulder and with a commanding tone of voice say:
"BOW YOUR HEAD WITH ME"

NOTE: Do not look at him when you say this, but <u>bow your own head first</u>. Out of the corner of your eye you will see him hesitate at first, and then as his resistance weakens, his head will come down. Bowing your head first causes terrific psychological pressure. Usually it is at this point that an individual will balk if he is unable to make a decision. Generally he will say, "I can't do it!" Some, however, will go all the way with you even though they have not made a genuine decision; usually the Holy Spirit gives discernment in such a case that you might deal with them accordingly.

When his head is bowed, say:

You: "Now just tell the Lord Jesus that you know you're a sinner, and that you want Him to come into your heart. Can you do that?" (Pause just a couple of seconds to give him a chance to pray

PAUSE ONLY BRIEFLY AFTER YOU GIVE THE INVITATION. THEN IF THE SUBJECT HESITATES TO ANSWER, URGE HIM WITH "BOW YOUR HEAD WITH ME!"

alone if he will—if there's no response, or he says, "I don't know how!" then you say:)

You: "All right, I'll help you—just follow me out loud, if you will." (Then, without any further delay, lead him something like this:)

"Dear Lord Jesus, I confess that I am a sinner, and I here and now open the door of my heart and invite you to come in. I now put my trust in you as my personal Saviour! Amen." (Pause after each phrase that he may follow easily).

NOTE: You have done all that is humanly possible to bring a person to a decision. You have presented Christ at his heart's door—you have asked him to invite Him in—you have used every technique and device to confront him with the reality of the decision—you have brought him to the place where he has had to say either, "Come into my heart, Lord Jesus" or "Go away, I don't want your Salvation." He has to take a stand one way or the other. Either he wants Christ or he doesn't. When an individual refuses to receive Christ, make sure that he understands what he has done. This is accomplished by confronting him with, "I haven't asked to come into your heart, have I? You're not refusing _me_, but the One who died for you."

Occasionally you will take a person all the way through the plan and when you come to the place where it is time to invite Jesus into

—48—

his heart, he will say, "I've already done that." Perhaps he has. If that is the case, then God has been using you to strengthen a little Babe.

AFTER THE PRAYER OF INVITATION, LOOK YOUR SUBJECT SQUARELY IN THE EYE AND ASK:

You: "Did you mean it when you asked the Lord Jesus to come into your heart?"

Most will answer: "Of course. I wouldn't have said it unless I meant it!"

You: "All right, you've opened the 'door', haven't you —and what did the Lord Jesus say He'd do if you'd open the door?"

Subject: "He said He'd come in!"

You: "Is He a liar?"

Subject: "No, He's not a liar."

You: "If you opened the door—and He said that He'd come in, and He's not a liar—where is He then?"

Subject: "He's in my heart."

You: "You see, it's not how you feel that tells you whether you're saved or not, but whether you believe God's Word or not. If you believe that Jesus has come into your heart because He cannot lie and because you have truly invited Him to come in, then you can know you are saved, because God has given you the faith to believe His Word!"

You: "Now, I'll ask you to do one more thing. Would you now just bow your head again, and this time, by yourself, say, 'Thank you, Lord, for the gift of eternal life'—just that much?"

NOTE: Experience has shown this to be a wonderful test. The Holy Spirit apparently will not allow a person to pray this prayer unless he has actually received the gift. It is only courtesy to say, "Thank you" for any gift that we have received. Once in a great while, a person will not want to pray this prayer. Though this is rare, one should be prepared for it. When it does occur, it is probably because the subject has gone through the plan just to get rid of you, or his decision has been made in his head and not in his heart. It is possible that he has failed to understand the message and was unable to actually make a decision. If you can discern this, then go through the steps once again. However, if he has understood the challenge clearly, do not press him further, but let the matter rest at this point.

Subject: "Thank you, Lord, for the gift of eternal life."

A part of your work is now completed. The leading of an individual to Christ is just the beginning in the obeying of the Great Commission which commands us to DISCIPLE men. The discipling is the all important task, of which personal evangelism is but the first step. Men must <u>meet</u> Christ before they can <u>follow</u> Him.

The person you have just led to Jesus is now on the road to discipleship. Your responsibility to him is not finished with his decision, though it may be the task of another to take him deeper into the things of the Christian life. As he stands before you now, he is just a helpless "new-born" babe. It is not thinkable that he should be left to shift for himself, any more that it is for a mother to leave her new-born infant to care for itself. This "new-born" babe in Christ is now a member of the church of Jesus Christ, and it becomes the full responsibility of the church to feed and care for his spiritual needs.

It is in this regard that the church functions in a supreme task. It is the church that has been commissioned to disciple the nations; and, as Christ's ordained means, the local assemblies are the only authorized institutions that can carry out the task. Soul-winning is a church function and should never be thought of as being carried on apart from the local church unless you are willing to assume the full responsibility for his training, for it is the church that provides the necessary elements for Christian growth. The church may be the one that meets in your home, or it may be the one that meets in the building at the corner, but the instructions would be the same in either case— <u>win</u> and <u>build</u> men for Jesus Christ.

As you look at your newly won babe, compassion should

—51—

flood your heart for him, as you now realize how desperately he needs to be cared for and trained. Somehow he must be encouraged to see his place in the community of the Redeemed of Christ and receive the encouragement that only the local church can provide. The family relationship provides a vivid illustration, and there is a true sense in which the church of Jesus Christ is one large family.

You: "Because you have received Christ into your heart, you are now a child of God. God is your Father now! Remember the verse we read: 'To as many as received Him, to them gave He power to become THE SONS OF GOD!' You are now a member of God's family, and you have many brothers and sisters; in fact, you are my Christian brother now."

You: "I do not know what kind of a family you are from, but there is nothing more wonderful than a happy family where each cares for the other and enjoys one another. But what kind of family life would there be, do you suppose, if we never talked to our father, but selfishly ignored him all the time—treating him as though he didn't exist—where he could say what he wanted to, but we would never speak to him—that surely wouldn't produce a very happy home, would it?"

Subject: "I don't think so."

You: "Neither can we be truly happy in the family of God if we refuse to talk to our Heavenly Father.

Our talking to God is prayer. Without that, it would be an abnormal family."

You: "Now suppose that in our family, no matter how much our father wanted to talk to us, we wouldn't listen to him, and no matter what he'd say, we would pay no attention—would that make a very happy family?"

Subject: "No, it wouldn't."

You: "Well, God our Father speaks to us through His Word, this Book. When we read it, we are listening to Him. As we talk to God through prayer, and as He speaks to us through the Bible, there is a beautiful fellowship between us continually."

You: "But the family we are talking about has brothers and sisters. There would be no real happiness in a family where we would just talk to our father but ignored the other members, would there?"

Subject: "No."

You: "That's why going to church is important. We have brothers and sisters that gather together at least once a week to greet one another and tell of the wonderful things that God has been doing in their lives. There Christians talk things over as a family and see how they can best care for one another, especially new Christians like yourself. Great joy comes in our Christian life as we learn how to live and work together as a happy family of Christians."

Continue: "The world doesn't like Christians too well, and we have to stick together and look out for one another. You know yourself that you never hear any of these things on the job or on the street; why, there the Lord's Name is only mentioned in profanity."

You: "It is in the church that we learn of the things Christ has done for us, and now you have the privilege of going to any church where Jesus Christ is truly worshipped and feeling as a part of the family gathered there. As a matter of fact I'd like to invite you to my church and to be able to introduce you to some of your Christian brothers and sisters. Going to church has nothing to do with your salvation. You already have that as a free gift, but you'll find it necessary to enjoy the Christian life to the fullest."

THE USE OF THE "B"-RATIONS AND BOOKLETS

Sometimes you can do nothing more than place these aids in the subject's hand, but it is much more satisfactory if there is time to give him just a bit of instruction concerning their use. Regarding the "B-Rations", you can say:

You: "Perhaps (Bill), in a little while after I'm gone, a thought like this will occur to you, 'That was a strange experience I had. A fellow comes along—tells me about Christ—and I bow my head and ask Jesus to come into my heart. Then he tells me that my sins are forgiven, and I'm on my way to Heaven . Surely there must be more to it than that; just opening my heart's door can't be enough to get me to Heaven'. When that happens, Bill, the only thing that will drive away your doubts is a promise from God's Word. This little packet that I am giving you contains four verses that will help you when those doubts come into your mind. They are on little cards so that you can carry them in your pocket and memorize them. It will amaze you how four little verses can give you so much assurance."

You: "And then, in the front of the booklet, there are a few pages which explain many of the things we have talked about. You'll not remember everything that I've said to you, and you'll find these remarks will refresh your memory.

Concerning the pamphlet:

You: "This little pamphlet will explain further the salvation that you received today. On each page there is some important fact of your salvation made very clear."

Concerning the Gospel of John:

You: "Today is your birthday—you became a child of God today. All of us like to keep track of our birthdays, and on the back page of this little

Gospel is a place to record the date and the decision that you have made today. You'll want to keep it as a record of the day you became a Christian."

NOTE: The subject won't mind writing his name in the space that is provided on the back page of the Gospel booklet if you explain to him that he is recording his decision and that it will be his own record for the future. It gives a further sense of the *transaction* that has taken place between him and God.

FINAL WORDS BEFORE YOU LEAVE THE SUBJECT

Ask him: "Now (subject's name), if someone were to ask you, 'Are you a Christian', what would you say?"

Subject: "I'd say, 'Yes, I am'."

You: "But, suppose he said, 'How do you know', how would you answer him?" (Sometimes the subject may pause, in which case you can ask him:)

You: "What did you ask Jesus to do?"

Subject: "To come into my heart."

You: "That's how you know—because you have asked the Lord to do the thing that He said He would do, and He cannot lie!"

These words in parting bring strength to the new Christian and are used as you take leave of him—in this way they are more likely to be remembered. So much has

THERE IS NO WAY TO CONCEAL THE JOY THAT COMES FROM
INTRODUCING A SOUL TO CHRIST.

happened and so much has been said that it is probable that he will remember very little of all the things mentioned. About all that he will be conscious of is that he has made a decision for Christ. This is the point you are trying to drive home!

H O W   T O   U S E   T H E   P L A N
READ IT — TRY IT — READ IT

It is not expected that you will memorize the dialogue that begins on page26 but you should become familiar with the procedure that is used in each step. You will find it helpful to learn well the transition from verse to verse. These lines have been carefully planned; and, if committed to memory, they will enable you to move smoothly from one verse to the next.

You have no doubt noticed already that the heart of this plan is a Person in whom is life eternal. The purpose of the plan is to get an individual to receive Him. SALVATION is receiving this Person.

TO DO THIS YOU FOLLOW FOUR DISTINCT STEPS:

1. You convince the subject that he is a sinner.

2. He learns   that his sin has already earned for him eternal separation from God.

3. You show him that he need not be separated from God for Jesus Christ has died for him, and because of this, God offers him the gift of eternal life through Christ.

—58—

4. You show him how he may receive this free gift and ask him to do so.

THIS IS ACCOMPLISHED BY USING FOUR VERSES:

1. Romans 3:23 — teaching the fact that <u>all men are sinners</u>.

2. Romans 6:23a — the fact that this sin has earned for men <u>the penalty of death</u>. (Eternal Separation)

   Romans 6:23b — the fact that God has a <u>free gift</u>.
   — that the gift is <u>eternal life</u> — which is the opposite of death.
   — that the gift is <u>in</u> a Person.

3. John 1:12 — that this <u>Person</u> needs <u>to be received</u> in order to have the gift.

4. Revelation 3:20 — that you receive this Person by <u>inviting Him</u> into your heart.

HOW TO USE THE FOUR VERSES:

Romans 3:23 — this verse is made effective by asking two questions:

1. "Have you ever told a lie in all your life?" Then hold up one finger in his line of vision as you ask,"How many lies does it take to make a liar?"

2. "If the Lord Jesus were standing right here be-

side you, would you say that you were as righteous as He?" — followed by, "Why not?"

Romans 6:23a — this is visualized with the illustration
of California's Law guaranteeing
wages to a worker.

Romans 6:23b — the "gift" is accentuated by noting
that a gift cannot be earned.
— the fact that the "gift" is <u>in</u> a Person is demonstrated by pretending
that the card is a $5 bill, and after
placing it in the New Testament,
offering it to the subject.

John 1:12 — the word "received" is the one we are
trying to make clear here. The difference
between believing and receiving is also
demonstrated with the card.

Revelation 3:20 — this verse requires the most in the
way of dramatic illustration. Three
definite things are done to make
the subject fully aware of the reality of the event:

1. Tapping his heart to indicate the
"door".

2. Asking him what he would say
in answer to a knock at the door.

3. Firmly laying your hand on his
shoulder accompanied by the
command to bow his head.

Your *questions* focus the subject's attention on the
thought.

Your *illustrations* make clear the meaning of the
verses.

Your *catch phrases* crystallize the central thought
you are expressing.

WARNING

There is need for caution at the decision point,
for the use of an unfortunate question can thwart
all that you hope to accomplish in bringing the
subject thus far. You will find yourself tempted
to ask, "Have you ever done that?" or again, "Have
you ever asked Christ to come into your heart?",
instead of challenging him with; "Will you ask Him
to come into your heart now!" In so doing the
subject is provided with an easy escape from the
conviction that is pressing upon him, for the simple
answer "yes", would put an end to your challenging work. Instead press him to receive Christ, and
leave the matter of any previous decision alone.
In all probability he will volunteer that information
anyway.

THE SUCCESS OF YOUR PLAN IS HEIGHTENED GREATLY BY YOUR USE OF THE PSYCHOLOGICAL TECHNIQUES

There are six that prepare the subject:

1. Your finger held just below his line of vision offers a suggestion that always provokes his response. This sharply drives home the fact that the subject is a liar and indicates to him that he himself has a need.

2. In having him reach for the card, he gets the sense of appropriating for himself that which you are talking about. Here the sense of *touch* is employed.

3. You *shatter* his dream world as you tap on his heart.

4. In the last step he says, "Come in" in response to your illustration of a friend at the door. This prepares him to say, "Come in" to the Lord Jesus at the moment of your invitation.

5. Your hand laid firmly on his shoulder, at the same instant that you command him to bow his head, gives you an *authority* that is difficult to resist.

6. The sight of your bowed head before him is almost *irresistible.*

THE PLACE OF PSYCHOLOGY IN SOUL WINNING

God has given us a unique tool called psychology that plays a very important part in soul winning today. Many who in the past have been afraid of the term are now excited as to the advantages that it gives the personal worker and the increased effectiveness that it affords in Christ's service.

One is not long engaged in the soul winning activity before he discovers that with many of his contacts for Christ, the very moment the spiritual subject is mentioned an almost desperate attempt is made to get up a protective smoke screen. There is an obvious desperation on the part of people to avoid the Person of Jesus Christ. They will say anything to keep you from confronting them with their responsibility to God. How they sputter and squirm; "I have my own ideas on religion"; "I go to church"; "I have a brother who's a missionary"; "I do the best I can and I believe that I'll get by all right". Were it not so tragic, one could almost laugh at the obvious frustration that occurs when it appears that the Lord is about to become the center of the conversation.

This "smoke screen" is due to the popularity of religion today. A religious wave is presently sweeping America to the place where it is now fashionable for radio announcers to conclude their broadcasts with Bible verses, while others find it opportune to end their programs with "God bless you" and other cliches. People are going to church in greater numbers than ever before, with the bulk of them remaining unsaved, yet becoming familiar with Christian talk. "Repentance", "Born Again", "Salvation" are no longer terms that belong to the saved alone, for even the man on the street is now conversant with them. Songs are more popular today if they have a sacred idea connected with them, for men are now quite willing to approve religion *at a distance,* but to talk of Christ's claim upon their lives is an altogether different matter.

It is because of this situation today that God has given us the unique tool of psychology. By means of this tool, the smoke screen can be pushed aside and the unsaved soul exposed to his needy condition. Instead of letting men hide behind their excuses and escape in their ignorance, we now have a means whereby we can bring them face to face with Christ. This does not invade the territory of the Holy Spirit for this is purely a human effort. It is as though we, by human hands, were to take a man by the shoulders and hold him in such a position that he would have to look at the Christ. The Holy Spirit's job is to make Christ real. Psychology's job is to make men face Him. The decision that men make is, of course their own, for neither psychology nor the Holy Spirit can interfere with that.

PRACTICE WITH OTHERS

After you have read the plan *several times* and have begun to get the "feel" of it, find someone who also is interested in soul-winning and practice together. In your practice master just those things that seem to form the bare outline. Even though the plan appears one way on the printed page, it will be so clothed with your own personality that it will soon become your own personal system. *Reading* and *practicing* are vital if you are to be "sharp." God uses us at moments when we least expect it; therefore, we must always watch and be ready. Remember what we have already noted of the worldly salesman—how that he practices daily to be effective.

PREPARATION

Nothing is so distressing as to have an opportunity to talk with someone about Christ and not have your New Testament at hand. There is just no way of knowing when the Holy Spirit will present us with the opportunity to introduce someone to Jesus and for this reason we must be constantly prepared. Sometimes a job started in the backyard ends with an over the fence conversation with the neighbor, or again, what first appeared to be a trip to the store might prove later to be a soul winning expedition if we are equipped for it.

It is a very wise policy to make sure that you never leave the house without first checking to see if you have your tools handy. The Lord has told us that He will make us "fishers of men" if we follow Him, and we need constantly to have our "tackle" ready for the moment He might alert us. It is a terrible burden upon our hearts when we think of the "Ones that got away."

Some find it expedient to keep an extra New

Testament in the car just in case that young high school lad they pick up is one that the Holy Spirit has selected for them to deal with. Your car by the way is a good place for "fishing"; here you have all the privacy you need and your passenger does feel some obligation to listen to what you have to say.

In any event, make it a practice to go no place without your New Testament. The frontiersmen of our early days felt half clothed if they did not have their "six-gun" strapped to their side; we soul winners ought to feel the same incompleteness when we are without our "Sword." This is a matter that needs the *greatest stress,* for it is a shame to let golden opportunities slip by simply because we haven't taken time to be prepared.

APPENDIX
IN DEFENSE OF THE USE OF REVELATION 3:20

Some may criticize your use of this verse as a salvation text, claiming that it more properly represents the excluded Christ seeking admittance to His church. A careful examination of the passage reveals that this is <u>NOT</u> the case.

1. Notice that this church is trusting in "uncertain riches," saying "I am rich . . . and have need of nothing" (Verse 17) and not trusting in the Person of Christ.

2. The church is in need of righteousness ("fine linen") and the Holy Spirit ("eye-salve to <u>anoint</u> your eyes") Verse 18.

3. Since Christ rebukes and reproves those whom He loves, these should know that they are not His own; therefore, they are exhorted to "repent." Verse 19.

4. The invitation is not delivered to the church, but rather to individuals. "If <u>any man</u> will open the door," Jesus says, clearly speaking of salvation for that is an individual matter. Verse 20. One man is not seen as opening the door of any church to Christ.

5. Jesus continues to speak to the individual, "He that overcometh . . ." "and who is <u>he</u> that overcometh but <u>he</u> that believeth that Jesus is the Christ."

The entire church is seen as the one characterizing that great apostasy of the last days, and as always there is Jesus' invitation to salvation, even to those found within the false church.

WHY YOU SHOULD USE A PLAN

Sears Roebuck & Company newly engaged in a house to house selling campaign, give to their salesmen a carefully prepared presentation or "pitch" as they call it. The salesman is expected to read it daily before he attempts to do that day's calling. The system that you now have in your hand is tremendously successful and will become a part of you the more you read it. You will notice its value as an effective tool when you try it —read it—and try it again. It is so easy to forget little details. They can only be recalled as you constantly brush up on your technique. Frequent reading keeps you "sharp."

If you have never entertained the idea of using a plan in soul-winning before, there are at least twelve advantages that you might consider:

1. It gives you a tremendous confidence that in turn produces boldness.

2. You never have to grope for words for you know always what you are going to say next.

3. You have the advantage of knowing what to expect from the subject with whom you are dealing.

4. You can control the conversation.

5. You are forced to stay on the subject and work systematically toward the one goal of the subject's salvation.

6. You are free to analyze the subject and study him instead of having to plan what you are going to say next.

7. Your plan is one that Jesus has used to bring hundreds to Himself.

8. You can bring one to a decision much faster.

9. You are prevented from becoming confused.

10. The subject develops confidence in you because you know what you are doing.

11. You do not need a lot of Scripture verses to accomplish the task.

12. Your mind is freed from the stress of planning your next move, and you will find that you are able to keep in touch with the Lord as well as explain the steps.

YOUR PLAN A FREEWAY

Our major cities are fast acquiring freeway systems to relieve the automobile congestion. These broad eight lane arteries permit vehicles to move in an uninterrupted flow across the busy towns and travel miles out into the suburbs without a single stop. It takes minutes today to cover the same ground that a few years ago took hours, because of the swift directness provided by the freeway. A man can be miles from the heart of town, but he knows that if he can get on that freeway, he'll rapidly come to his destination.

Your familiar plan gives you the same facility as a personal worker. No matter what the conversation is about, a worker knows that if he can once bring the subject to the question, "Are you interested in spiritual things?", he is at once on the freeway! He knows that in a short time the subject will be face to face with Christ, for once he is on that familiar plan, the covering of the necessary distance becomes almost automatic. In the space of minutes the worker is asking, "Will you let Him come into your heart?"

FOLLOW-UP WORK

As has been hinted earlier, the "follow-up" work is as vital as the actual "soul-winning." A special booklet is being prepared and will soon be ready for distribution which will enable you to skilfully carry on a home ministry of 10 lessons that should thoroughly ground a new Christian in the fundamental truths of the Christ life. Person to person is Jesus' way in both "soul-winning" and "soul-building" even though you are working through your church.

It is this pastor's hope that the Lord will use the plan in your hands to bring many souls to Him. A single worker can bring a tremendous number to Christ over a period of years — know-how is vital in any work, but it is most important to us in the Lord's work. May God richly bless you as you apply this KNOW HOW in His service.

C. S. Lovett

RECORD FOR PRAYER AND FOLLOW UP

"YOUR JOY AND CROWN" Phil. 4:1

NAME _____

ADDRESS _____

PHONE _____ DATE _____

WHERE _____

REMARKS _____

NAME _____

ADDRESS _____

PHONE _____ DATE _____

WHERE _____

REMARKS _____

RECORD FOR PRAYER AND FOLLOW UP

"YOUR JOY AND CROWN" Phil. 4:1

NAME _____

ADDRESS _____

PHONE _____ DATE _____

WHERE _____

REMARKS _____

NAME _____

ADDRESS _____

PHONE _____ DATE _____

WHERE _____

REMARKS _____

RECORD FOR PRAYER AND FOLLOW UP

"YOUR JOY AND CROWN" Phil. 4:1

NAME _____

ADDRESS _____

PHONE _____ DATE _____

WHERE _____

REMARKS _____

NAME _____

ADDRESS _____

PHONE _____ DATE _____

WHERE _____

REMARKS _____

RECORD FOR PRAYER AND FOLLOW UP

"YOUR JOY AND CROWN" Phil. 4:1

NAME _____

ADDRESS _____

PHONE _____ DATE _____

WHERE _____

REMARKS _____

NAME _____

ADDRESS _____

PHONE _____ DATE _____

WHERE _____

REMARKS _____
